DATE DUE

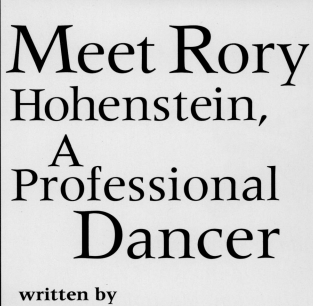

Meet Rory
Hohenstein, A Professional Dancer

written by
JILL D. DUVALL

photographs by
LILI DUVALL

Reading Consultant
LINDA CORNWELL
Learning Resource Consultant
Indiana Department of Education

CHILDREN'S PRESS®   *A Division of Grolier Publishing*
New York • London • Hong Kong • Sydney • Danbury, Connecticut

Dedicated to Deborah and Michael Hohenstein and Rory's grandparents

Special thanks to Madame Vinogradova, Deputy Artistic Director, and the Kirov Academy of Ballet, Ms. Dellas-Thornton, Mr. Hoffman, and Gary Pate

Library of Congress Cataloging-in-Publication Data
Duvall, Jill.
Meet Rory Hohenstein, a professional dancer / written by Jill D. Duvall ; photographs by Lili Duvall ; reading consultant, Linda Cornwell.
    p.   cm. — (Our neighborhood)
    Summary: Describes the life of a teenage dancer and shows how his practice and hard work pay off during a performance at the Kirov Academy in Washington, D.C.
    ISBN 0-516-20312-6 (lib. bdg.)—ISBN 0-516-26149-5 (pbk.)
    1. Hohenstein, Rory—Juvenile literature. 2. Dancers—United States—Biography—Juvenile literature. [1. Dancers. 2. Occupations.] I. Duvall, Lili, ill. II. Title. III. Series: Our neighborhood.
    GV1785.H58D88   1997
    792.8'028'092—dc20

                                                        96-34906
                                                           CIP
                                                            AC

Photographs ©: Paolo Galli, courtesy of the Kirov Academy of Ballet: 30-31; all other photos: Lili Duvall.
Makeup by Amy Sue Mechalek: 12-17.

In the dance studio, Rory Hohenstein starts working very early. He is a professional dancer. He must practice many hours every day.

Ms. Dellas is Rory's dance teacher.
She shows him a ballet position.

The whole class gets ready to dance.

Ms. Dellas tells her class that professional dancers are always learning new things.

She was a ballerina for many years. Rory is happy to have such a good teacher.

Rory does jazz, tap, and ballet.

But no matter what kind of dancing Rory does, he must wear the right shoes.

They must fit perfectly.

Dancers stretch before they begin dancing. Ouch! Rory's friend helps him stretch his legs.

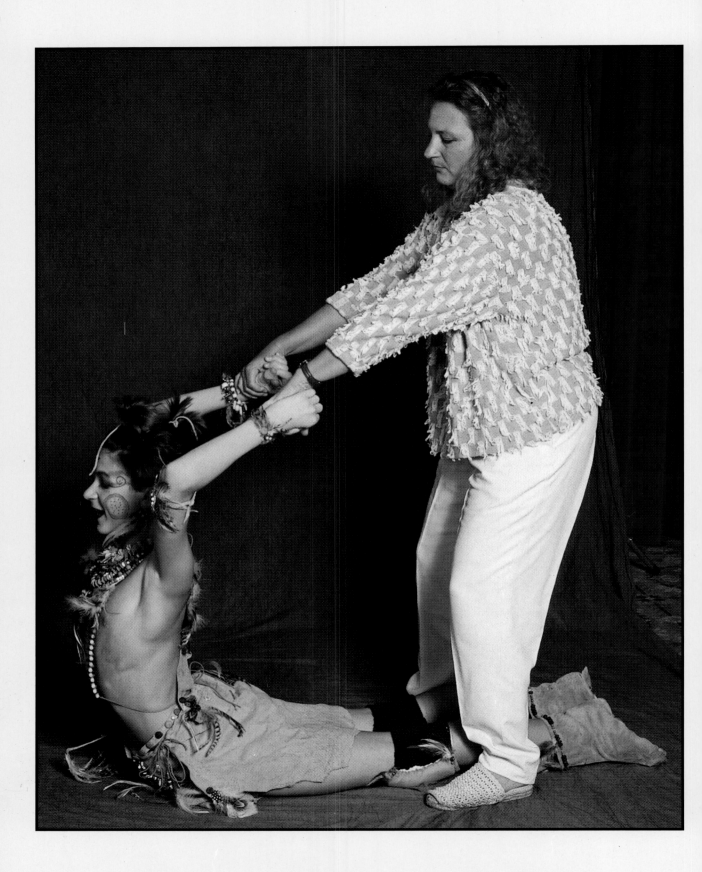

Rory's mom helps him stretch his back and arms. Every one of his muscles has to be very strong to do such a big kick!

When Rory performs, he acts many different parts.

Every part has its own costume.

Rory created a dance about a fierce warrior. He and his mom made the costume.

Rory goes to a special dance school.

Just like other kids his age, Rory
studies many subjects.

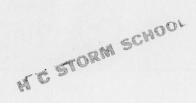

At the end of the day, it is time for fun, family, and food. But the next day, it will be time for practice again!

Rory practices with other dancers for an important performance. They are going to perform "The Nutcracker."

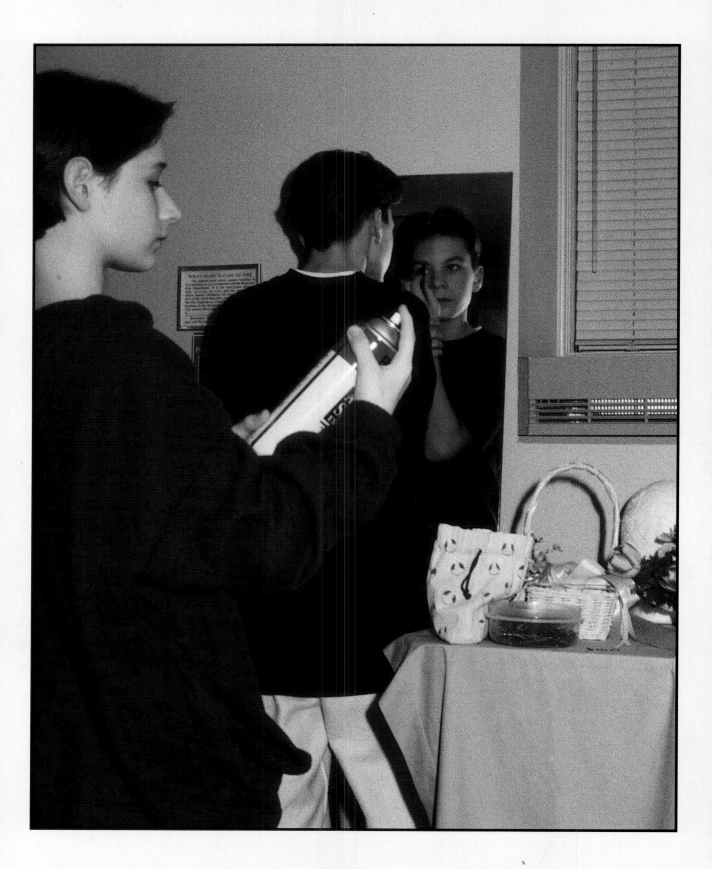

Dress rehearsal is the final practice before a performance. Rory must put on makeup and then get into his costume.

The dancers wait offstage to rehearse their parts.

Rory's part is the Balloon Man.

After the dress rehearsal, the dancers join hands and practice their bows.

27

Performance time is here! After lots of hard work, Rory is excited to get on stage. The audience is arriving. Soon the curtain will go up . . .

29

. . . and Rory will dance.

Meet the Photographer and the Author

Lili Duvall decided when she was in her teens that she wanted to take pictures. She is now a professional photographer and taking pictures of children is her favorite work. Her home and studio are in Maryland.

Jill Duvall, Lili's writing partner, is also her mother. Jill likes living near Washington, D.C., because much of her studying and writing is about the government. Jill feels that writing is very important and even takes her writing to the beach!